Magick of Love:

Spells to find and keep a lover & heal a broken relationship.

By: Lady Lillyth

Table of Contents

All You Need is Love

John Lennon was famous for saying "All you need is love." We all know we need other essentials but having love makes our journey easier. Many people spend a great deal of time, and money, trying to find it. You can see this by all of the dating sites that are constantly being created. But remember, love comes in many different forms and can be found in many different places. You should not overlook the love of your friends and family. They can certainly help to see you through the dark times and celebrate the good ones with you.

Sometimes what you need to find true love is just a little magic. (It certainly can't hurt!) This book of spells can help you on your journey to finding the love that will make you happy. It contains spells for attraction -- making other people attracted to you and attracting love to your life. You will also find spells for keeping love, fixing a damaged relationship or ending one that has gone terribly wrong.

If you are beginner to spell craft, there is a section to help you get started. You will find tips on setting up sacred space, the tools you need, how to prepare yourself for working magic and how to cast a circle. If you are a novice, you can skip these sections and go straight to the spells.

A word of warning: You should never cast a spell directed at a particular person, as this goes against the ethics of spell casting. When people find out, I am Wiccan the first thing they ask me for is a love spell. I strongly suggest that you do not cast any spell using a specific person in mind. Sure, you may make them fall in love with you, but later you may come to realize they are not a good match. Now instead of a life partner you have created a stalker. You are better off using magic to bring love into your life. Have faith that the universe will bring you the love you need, even if it comes in a package you did not expect.

Just using the spells in this book will not bring your true love knocking at your door unless the postman or FEDEX delivery person is your true love. You have to put yourself out there. You have to be willing to strike up a conversation with an interesting stranger or go to places where people are. You have to open your heart and mind to the possibility of love, and it will find you.

The Inner Workings of a Spell

Spells work to manifest desires or changes in your life. They are similar to a prayer and can be simple or complex. The way they work is to speak to your subconscious to bring about the change you desire. The subconscious mind does not understand written or verbal language. Instead, you need to speak to it by using symbols. The tools and ingredients used in spells are simply symbols.

Spells work in two ways; from the inside out or the outside to the inside. The ingredients or tools you use are activated by your words and actions. Simple spells may require no more than a few words, eating the ingredients or taking a bath. Complex spells usually require the casting of a circle, magical tools and invocations. Understanding how the various ingredients work will make your spells more effective.

Baths

Magical baths represent the elements of earth and water. Take a magic bath when you want to work on either the physical body or your emotions. Baths work best when taken on a full or new moon. Prepare the required ingredients and add to a tub of warm to hot water. You should soak in the bath for at least fifteen minutes. Take this time to clear your mind and visualize your desire. Do not rinse off or shower for at least 24 hours after performing a magic bath.

Candles

Candles are used to represent the element of fire, which influences actions. You want to use candles when making a request. Candles can be carved with symbols or anointed with oils that correspond with the request. You can also surround the candles with herbs or flowers that correspond to your desire.

Incense

Incense represents the air element is best used for spells to influence thought processes. Incense comes in many different forms; cone, stick, or loose. When using loose incense you will need a fireproof bowl or cauldron and small charcoal briquettes.

Oils

Oil represents the water element is used for spells involving the emotions. They can be a single scent or a combination of different oils that create the desired magical effect. Oils are used to anoint candles, the body and when making talismans.

Moon Cycles

Moon cycles effect the timing of spells. Two cycles of the moon are waxing and waning. The waxing moon starts on the new moon and ends on the full moon. The moon is getting larger so you would perform spells of increase. The waning moon is the cycle when the moon gets smaller. This cycle begins on the full moon and ends on the new moon. During the waning moon is when you perform spells of banishing or decrease.

Moon Phases

The moon has three phases that coincide with the three faces of the Goddess. The new moon corresponds with the Maiden and is the best time to work spells to create something new. The Mother is represented by the full moon. During this phase is the time to work spells to bring something to fruition. The dark moon corresponds to the Crone. The dark moon occurs one day before the new moon. This phase is when you should work spells for wisdom or an ending.⬚

Preparing Yourself for Magic

Before casting your first spell, there are a few things you should do first. This chapter will give you the basics to get you started. A lot of books exist on this subject, but the best thing to do is find out what works for you. One of the many wonderful things about the spellcraft is that you can make it uniquely yours. Follow your beliefs, your heart and the one basic rule: Any ye harm none, do what ye will.

Tools of the Trade

Many beginners think they need to have a lot of tools before they start. You do not. Tools do not make the magic work; they are only symbols. If you do not have a chalice, you can use a wine glass or coffee cup from your cupboard. You can substitute any fireproof vessel for a cauldron. If you are going to buy any tools before you begin I would highly suggest you purchase an athame, as this, in my opinion, is the most important one.

An athame is a double-edged knife, or letter opener will work. You will not be using it to cut much of anything. The athame is a symbol and most often used to direct energy or power. The other item I would recommend is a good mortar and pestle. After collecting your tools, they need to be consecrated for magical purposes before you use them.

A number of ways exist to do this and depends on your path or personal beliefs. I consecrate my tools by leaving them under a full moon overnight, but again this is a personal preference. If the item is not new, I wash it with saltwater before placing it in the moonlight, to remove all of the energy left by the previous owner. How you choose to consecrate your tools is up to you, the purpose of doing this is to "mark" them as sacred objects.

Ritual or Magical Cleansing

You do not want to enter your circle without cleansing yourself first. Doing so would be like going to work without bathing or brushing your hair. A quick way to do this is by smudging yourself with a sage stick. Light the sage and using your open hand waft the smoke over your body, front to back. Another way is to bathe in a tub of salted water.

While in the tub, use your hands to wash away all negative thoughts and energies from your mind, body and psychic areas. Take a few minutes to visualize yourself surrounded by blue-white light that is purifying, protecting and energizing you. When you feel ready, leave the bath and dress in something that makes you feel comfortable and powerful.

Consecrating Sacred Space

After cleansing the body and the mind, you will need to cleanse the area where you will be working your magic. Like everything in spell crafting, you can do this in a number of different ways. Try experimenting with a few until you find the one that you like best.

Smudging the area with a sage stick is a simple way to cleanse the area. Walk doesil (clockwise) around the area and banish all negative energies while wafting the smoke from the stick around the area. You can sprinkle salt water, use incense or a combination of both. The purpose is to remove the negative and designate the space as sacred. Once done, you will be ready to cast your circle.

You Must Believe

One of the first things I tell anyone who wants to learn the craft is that they must believe. When you cast any spell, you are releasing your wants and desires into the universe. 90% of all magic comes from the belief that the spell you are casting will work. You cannot "think" it will work or "hope" it will work, you have to "know" it will.

You cannot "play" with magic or "dabble" in it. Doing so will cause your spell to rebound in untold ways. You have to believe with all of your heart that the spell will bring you what you want it to. This belief is why it is so important that you are specific about what you want. When asking for love in your life, be specific about the kind of love you want. If you are asking for a partner, describe him or her in detail, without using the name.

Circle Casting 101

Before casting your circle, set up your altar or work space in the area you have created. If you do not have an altar, the coffee or end table works just fine. Gather all of your spell ingredients together. Make sure you have followed all of the steps in the previous chapter. Remove all distractions from your sacred area, turn off the TV and the ringer on your phone. If you have children, you may want to wait until they are in bed before you begin.

Not to be repetitive, but casting a magic circle can be done in at least 101 different ways. You can go to the bookstore or online and find more detailed instructions on how to cast your circle; these are just the basic steps.

When casting a magic circle, always do so in a clockwise direction. Many people who practice magic know the number 3 is very powerful, so walk around your circle at least three times. You may want to chant or recite an incantation used for casting a circle. Try a couple of different methods that appeal to you until you find one that makes you comfortable.

Some people call on the guardians of the watchtowers and some use the elements represented by the cardinal points. Some will set symbols of the elements at each cardinal point and some do not. There is no rule set in stone on how to cast a spell or a circle. The idea is to invite the spirits or elements you are comfortable with to bless your circle and the work you will do within it.

For example, I like to bring joy and light into all of my magical workings. When I begin casting my circle, I dance around the area three times. I call upon the elements and use a bowl of salt for north, a candle for south, incense for east and a bowl of water for west. North represents Earth, South is Fire, East is Air and the West represents Water. I invite each of the elements to join me and bless me while in the circle. I also light a white candle in the center for the Goddess and ask for her blessing. Over time, I have found that this is the method that I like best.

Once the circle is cast and blessed you can begin your spell. Follow the directions and be sure to visualize what you desire. When you have completed the spell, you need to close the circle. When closing the circle, repeat the opening steps but work widdershins (or counterclockwise). Thank the Goddess and the elements for joining you and release them, and then walk or dance around the area in the opposite direction.

After any magical working be sure to rest and replenish yourself. Spell casting can use a lot of energies both physical and mental. Have a light snack and spend some time meditating or relaxing with an activity that you enjoy. Then get ready for the universe to deliver what you requested.

Simple Foods Become Simple Spells

Many common fruits, vegetables and other foods can become edible spells. These spells are a quick and tasty way to accomplish your desires. While preparing them and eating them be sure to visualize your goal.

Food for Love

Anise is a licorice-flavored herb and has many magical uses. To attract a lover, use a red licorice whip for this quick spell. While tying the knot in the whip, verbally say, "I want to find a lover who is ____" (fill in the blank with the quality or qualities you are looking for). Place your thumb and middle finger on the knot and repeat the phrase three times. When finished eat the licorice.

Eating barley on a Friday will attract love to you. Use it to make a soup or stew or bake it into bread. If the taste of barley is not appealing, you may also sprinkle raw barley on your altar as an offering to Venus.

Cabbage can be used to bring love to you. Use a whole red cabbage and bless it before you use it. To perform the blessing; hold the cabbage in both hands and speak a prayer of blessing making sure to specify what your goal is. In matters of the heart, Venus is one goddess you can call on. When the blessing is complete cut your name in the head of cabbage before using. You should cook the cabbage whole and eat it or use it in another recipe.

Since dates belong to Venus, they carry properties of love. Pit the dates and roll them in powder sugar. Eating these tasty treats help you to remove the obstacles that are preventing you from finding the love you want.

Honey is a favorite of all love goddesses. Use honey in a magical bath to attract love. Add ¼ cup honey to a tub of warm water. Soak for at least 15 minutes; be sure to spend the time thinking of all of the qualities that you would like to have in a partner or lover.

Use a honeydew melon to cast a wish spell. You will want to cast this spell on a full moon. Wrap your arms around the melon and hold it close to your heart. Close your eyes and wish for the love that you want. Cut the melon in half. Eat one-half yourself and leave the other half as an offering to the goddess, preferably under a tree.

Marjoram is one herb you can use for love in different ways. Add it to a favorite recipe and serve to family and friends to bring love and happiness to all. Another way to use marjoram is to burn a spring of the herb before you say, "I love you" to your partner for the first time. By doing this, you are sure to hear the words returned to you.

Marzipan is a sweet confection made from sugar and almonds. Pick a Friday, on, or before, a full moon to make some marzipan and shape it into a flower. Make a wish on the flower and either place it on your altar or under a tree as an offering.

Sugar added to love spells, can help to bring you quicker results. Word of warning, when adding sugar to a spell be sure to use only the raw, purest form. Refined sugar can bring you unwanted karmic consequences. You can sprinkle powdered sugar on a pink candle to make another sweet on you.

Food for Passion

These foods act as aphrodisiacs. Use them when you want to add a little spice to your sex life.

Arugula was considered by the ancient Romans to be an aphrodisiac. To up the passion in your relationship, serve a salad made from arugula and tomatoes. Add a pinch of basil for a heterosexual couple, replace the basil with mozzarella cheese for a gay couple or add a splash of tomato juice for lesbian couples.

Serve the vegetable asparagus with hollandaise or white sauce with dinner. Be sure to eat the asparagus from the top down to the stem in order for it to be effective.

Basil correlates with the god Mars. This herb will increase passion or lust. Add it to favorite recipes to awaken the sexual appetite. Burn basil incense to stimulate sexual pleasure. Place dried basil under your bed to bring the passion back to your relationship.

Blackberries are a favorite of the goddess Venus. Eating the berries or jam before sex will heighten the pleasure and deepen the bond between lovers. Use wisely as blackberries are known to bring out the wild side of a person's personality.

Carrots are not only good for your eyesight but eating them will also give you more energy, willpower and sexual stamina. To inspire lust in your relationship eat carrot seeds on a Tuesday.

Hearts of palm is a vegetable that can be eaten to incite passion. Eat three stalks on a Sunday or Friday to increase your allure and stamina. Add the stalks to a salad and serve to the person you are interested in to start a love affair.

Onions are also a food of love. Many people believe that eating onions will increase a man's virility. Adding red onions to a recipe will encourage lust while using purple onions will ensure seduction.

The scent of the vanilla bean can be used to awaken sexual appetites. Burn vanilla incense or add a few drops of the pure extract to potpourri and place in the bedroom. You can also spray on vanilla perfume before going to bed to encourage your partner.

Food for relationships

Use these food to strengthen or end an existing relationship. You can also use food to solve problems in your current relationship.

Cranberries can be used to strengthen the bond between partners or to end a relationship. To deepen the bond with your partner drink cranberry juice together during the dark moon. To end a relationship, place a circle of the berries around a black candle. Light the candle and repeat the names of the people involved. Perform this ritual until you achieve the desired results.

You can use the spice cumin to keep your partner faithful. If your partner is cheating sprinkle powdered cumin in their shoes to keep them at home. Another way to prevent them from straying is to sprinkle cumin seeds under their pillow to prevent them from thinking of someone else.

Peach pits can be used to keep your partner from straying. Dry and crush the pits. Sprinkle the powdered peach pits on a red male or female candle in which you have carved your partner's name. Light the candle and let it burn out in a safe place. Put the melted candle wax under their side of the bed.

The flowers and the fruit of oranges symbolize committed love. Rub white or red candles with orange essential oil to strengthen love and commitment spells. You can also surround the candles used in a spell with dried orange peels.

Bake and serve your partner a rhubarb pie to promote loyalty and fidelity. You can also use rhubarb in relationship spells to help solve domestic problems.

Rice is considered to be a spiritual grain. We throw rice at married couples as a fertility blessing. You can use raw rice to encourage a marriage proposal. To create the marriage spell you need to place a picture of you and your partner in a jar. Add a cup of rice and the peel of one orange. Seal the jar with the melted wax of a pink candle. Place under your bed and shake the jar once a night until your partner proposes.

Draw Love to You

In order to find love, you need to be sure that your heart is open to receive it. You can use this simple spell to open your heart and mind to the prospect of love. Cast this spell on a Friday during a waxing moon.

Spell ingredients:

1 pink candle

12 inch length of crimson colored embroidery floss

3 gold colored buttons

To cast the spell:

Cast a protective circle and invite the quarters to join and bless you.

Place the pink candle in the middle of your altar and light it.

Begin by visualizing your heart chakra as a small rosebud. This bud has not begun to blossom yet but is tightly closed.

Place your palms down on the ground in front of you and release all of your fear and anxiety into Mother Earth.

Repeat the rose visualization only now the rosebud has opened slightly.

Take the embroidery floss and string the first button on to it. Tie a knot while repeating the charm:

My past loves are lessons learned in time.

String the second button on the floss, tie and knot and repeat:

I am present now and love who I have become.

Repeat with the third button and charm:

My heart is open to receive the love that is mine.

Close your eyes and see the rosebud has bloomed and opened.

Snuff the candle and close the circle.

Keep your charm under your mattress.

Strengthen Your Appeal

People are more drawn to you when you exude an air of confidence. Use this charm any time you want to attract others to you or your cause. This spell is best cast on a Tuesday during a full or waxing moon.

Spell ingredients:

Copper jewelry wire

Jewelry glue

Small clear quartz stone

Small carnelian stone

Small rose quartz stone

To cast the spell:

Cast your circle and invite the quarters.

Begin by empowering each of the three stones. Hold the clear quartz between your palms and chant the incantation three times:

I am light.

Hold the carnelian stone between your palms and chant the incantation three times:

I am radiant.

Hold the rose quartz between your palms and chant the incantation three times:

I am love.

Arrange the stones in a cluster. Use the jewelry glue to hold them together. Wait for the cluster to dry for a few minutes.

Take a piece of the copper wire and wrap it around the gemstone cluster. You may wrap the wire in any pattern that is pleasing to you. Focus on the intent of the charm while you are wrapping it with the wire. Be sure to create a loop from the wire at the top of the charm.

Thank the quarters for their help and participation and then close the circle.

Let your gemstone charm dry completely.

Once it is dry it is ready to be strung on a chain or cord of your choosing. Wear this charm whenever you need an added boost to make you more attractive to others.

Invite Love In

Casting love spells can be tricky. This spell works to bring love into your life without imposing on anyone's free will. You should cast this spell outside under a full moon.

Spell ingredients:

1 pink candle

1 plate

Rose petals or rosebuds

Piece of rose quartz or amethyst

Scrying mirror or dark bowl filled with water

To cast the spell:

First prepare yourself. You should make yourself look as attractive as possible. Shower and do your hair and makeup. Pretend that you are getting ready to go on that first date.

Take all of the ingredients outside with you. Now, cast your circle and call the quarters.

Place the pink candle on the plate and place the rose petals or rosebuds around the candle.

Hold the gemstone in your hands. Close your eyes and visualize yourself happy and loved. Focus on what it would feel like to be held by your perfect partner. Try to actually feel their arms around you.

Open your eyes and light the candle. Repeat the following charm:

Someplace where I cannot see

Lives the one who's right for me

Long I've waited, long I've yearned

As hours passed and seasons turned.

In this time and in this space

I ask to see my lover's face

Send to me the match that's true

Or bring me where I'll catch his/her view

Attract to me the love that's meant

The person who is heaven-sent

For good of all and with free will

My wish for love I now fulfill.

Use the scrying mirror or bowl of water and concentrate to see the face of the one who is meant for you.

Seven Day Candle Spell

When you know who you want as a partner this spell can be used to give them a little push in your direction. Caution, make sure this is the person you want to be attached to as it is much more difficult to break a love spell than it is to cast one. This spell takes seven days to complete. You should begin the spell on a Friday during the waxing moon.

Spell ingredients:

1 white or gold candle for a man

Tool for carving candles

Piece of green cloth

1 green candle for attraction

1 black or silver candle for a woman

To cast the spell:

Cast your circle and call the quarters.

Use your carving tool and mark the two candles representing you and the other person.

Mark the green candle into seven equal parts.

Place the male candle on the right side of your altar and the female on the left side, about twelve inches apart.

Place the green candle in between the other two, slightly behind them.

Focus on the person you desire.

Light the candle representing you first, then the other person and finally the green candle.

Now sit quietly and visualize yourself with the person you desire.

Let the candles burn down to the first mark on the green candle.

Snuff out the candles in the order that you lit them.

On day two, move the candle slightly closer together.

Repeat the steps above, starting with focusing on the other person. Light the candles in the same order as before.

Continue repeating the above steps. By day seven the candles should be touching. On day seven let the candles burn themselves out. Wrap the wax in the green cloth and keep in a safe place.

Lust for Me

Couples in a long term relationship can find themselves in a rut eventually. The love is still strong, but that special spark in the bedroom can start to get dim. If both people are Pagan then perform the spell together. Cast this spell on a Friday during the full or new moon.

Spell ingredients:

1 red candle

Patchouli essential oil

Rose petals, red and white

Sensual massage oil (choose a scent that is sexy to you)

Sexy underwear

To cast the spell:

Bathe first and put on the sexy underwear.

Cast your circle and invite the quarters. Call on the goddess Aphrodite to join and bless you.

Sprinkle the rose petals on your altar and around your circle.

Anoint yourself with the massage oil.

Anoint the candle with the oil rubbing from the ends towards the center. Place the candle on the altar and light it.

Visualize you and your partner in whatever positions or fantasies that you find sexy.

When you are ready, repeat the incantation:

My body is a temple

Blessed by Aphrodite

My heart is filled with passion

Vibrant, sweet and mighty

Fill my days with loving

And my nights with playful fun

Let moonlight find me naked

Our bodies joined as one

I welcome sex and sensual play

Embracing love's new measure

Together we will find our way

And rediscover pleasure

Thank the goddess and the quarters and close the circle.

Allow the candle to burn out safely. Do something to encourage sex with your partner.

Ignite the Energy of Romance

Romance is easy when you are at the beginning of a relationship. Keeping the romance alive over time takes a bit more work. You can use this spell to rekindle the spark. If your partner is also Pagan, the two of you should perform the spell together. The best time to cast this spell is on a Friday during the full or waxing moon.

Spell ingredients:

1 pink candle

Jasmine essential oil

Pink roses or other pink flowers that appeal to you

Piece of rose quartz

Symbols of romance (a picture of the two of you kissing, a lipstick kiss on a piece of paper or other item that makes you think of romance)

To cast the spell:

Cast your circle and invite the quarters. You may also ask Aphrodite to join and bless you.

Anoint the candle with the essential oil rubbing from the top to the bottom. Place it on your altar with the rose quartz and romantic symbols. Arrange the flowers around the other items on the altar.

Light the candle. Hold a flower in either hand and while focusing on your intention to be more romantic, repeat the incantation three times.

> Love like a flower
>
> Beautiful and delicate
>
> Blossom from a gentle touch
>
> Bloom from sweet attention
>
> Romance like the sun
>
> Will nurture my love
>
> And help it to grow
>
> As two into one

Thank the quarters, and Goddess if you invoked her, and close the circle.

Allow the candle to burn out safely. Place the rose quartz near your bed.

Kindle the Passion

Sometimes a love relationship will lose its spark when two people have been together for a while. Passion is part of the reason the two of you got together in the beginning and you just need to rekindle it again. You can use this spell to find that lost passion for each other. This spell is best cast on a Friday during the full or new moon.

Spell ingredients:

2 red candles

Jasmine essential oil or incense

Wooden bowl

2 cups rose petals

½ cup of dried orange peels

Symbols of passion (massage oil, pictures of couples in intimate situations)

To cast the spell:

Prepare yourself first by bathing and dressing in a sensual fashion.

Cast your circle and invite the quarters.

If you are using essential oil, anoint the candle by rubbing the oil from the center to the ends. Place the candles on either side of your altar and light them. If using incense, place to the right side of the altar and light it.

Place the symbols of intimacy on your altar between the candles.

Mix the rose petals and orange peel in the wooden bowl. Inhale the fragrance and visualize the type of passion you want in your relationship.

When you are ready repeat the incantation:

> Magic of the sensual kind
>
> I summon now to be my own
>
> Melding body, melding mind
>
> A quiet time for us alone.

Let us join in passion's dance

> A moment out of life's fast pace
>
> A kiss, a touch, a loving glance
>
> Each other's arms a sacred space.

Grant us intimacy filled with love

Bless us with a shared desire

As below and so above

Rekindle now our passion's fire.

Thank the quarters and close the circle.

Allow the candles and incense to burn out in a safe place. Sprinkle your enchanted rose petals on or around your bed.

Bind a Love to You

Falling in love is easy; it's the staying in love that is hard. Maintaining a good relationship takes work. But certainly a little magic help could not hurt once in a while. You can use this spell to strengthen a love relationship and bind your partner to you.

Spell ingredients:

1 apple with no spots or bruises

1 piece of paper

Edible ink

A pair of scissors

A handful of toothpicks

Sugar

To cast the spell:

Cleanse and prepare yourself, then create your sacred space.

Cast your circle and call the quarters.

Concentrate on your relationship being stronger.

Cut the apple in half.

Write your name and the name of your partner on the paper with the edible ink.

Cut the paper so that it is the same size as the apple. Then place the paper between the apple halves.

Use the toothpicks to fasten the halves together while reciting this charm:

Together we are bound

Me, in love with you,

You, in love with me.

May all our words and actions

Be a reflection of our love.

Blessed Be.

Sprinkle the apple with sugar. The Sugar represents the energy of love.

Close the circle and release the quarters.

Bake the apple at 350 degrees until both halves bake together.

While the apple is baking be sure to take the time to ground and center yourself.

Complete the spell by each of you eating half the apple.

Word of warning, a spell of this nature should not be used casually. Before performing this charm think long and hard if the partner you are with is truly the partner for you. If you should decide later that this is not your true love, you will have trouble shaking this person. Binding spells are not easy to break.

Good Marriage Spell

A good marriage requires commitment and dedication from both partners. You will also need good communication and a balanced relationship with both partners sharing responsibilities equally. This spell can be used to achieve a good marriage or can be used for a committed relationship too. If both partners are Pagan, they should both work the spell together. The best time to cast this spell is on a Friday during a full or waxing moon.

Spell ingredients:

1 pink candle

1 blue candle

Symbol of your marriage (wedding ring, wedding picture or picture of you two together)

Cardamom essential oil

To cast the spell:

Cast your circle and invite the quarters. You may also call on Hera the goddess of marriage.

Anoint the candles with the essential oil rubbing from the center to the ends.

Light the candle and place on the altar along with your marriage symbol.

If you are working alone, visualize you and your partner in fun, loving circumstances. If the two of you are working together, take this time to communicate your wants and needs and discuss your plans for the future.

When you are ready repeat the incantation, if working together the two of you should take turns repeating alternating lines:

> God and Goddess
>
> As you are joined with each other
>
> So I am joined with _____(NAME)
>
> In faith and hope and love

Help us to work together

> Toward a happy, healthy relationship
>
> Balanced and equal
>
> In work and compromise and love

Let our union be harmonious

> Productive, caring and filled with joy
>
> And let us overcome life's difficulties

With cooperation, communication and love

God and Goddess

Watch over this union

And let it grow stronger every day

With passion and joy and love

So mote it be.

Snuff out the candles and close the circle.

Domestic Bliss

Every marriage or relationship will face some type of problem now and then. Maintaining a good relationship takes work and dedication. Sometimes a little magical help is called for. Make and burn this incense to help clear the air during or after an argument. This spell will help to bring peace and harmony back to the relationship. The best time to perform this spell is on a Friday during the waxing moon.

Spell Ingredients:

2 white candles

Tool for carving candle

3 tablespoons rose hips

3 tablespoons fennel

3 tablespoons lavender

3 tablespoons rosemary

1 small bottle

Pentacle for the altar

Mortar and pestle

To cast the spell:

Cast your circle and call the quarters.

Place 1 white candle in the center of your altar. Place the pentacle below the white center candle.

With the carving tool, carve the following symbols around the second white candle:

A crescent moon, facing left, for harmony and sensitivity in the home

Mercury symbol for communication

Venus symbol for love

Rune symbol for Ken for receptivity

Rune symbol for Mannaz for cooperation

Rune symbol for Wyn for harmony

Light the center candle first. Next, light the carved candle from the center candle and repeat:

This flame burns for a loving, peaceful home.

Place the carved candle in a holder to the left of your altar. Place the mortar and pestle on the right side of the altar.

Hold each herb, individually over the pentacle and recite the corresponding line for each before adding to the mortar:

I call upon you rose hips for kindness and love

I call upon you fennel for protection of the marriage (relationship)

I call upon you lavender for peace in the home

I call upon you rosemary for love and blessings in the home

Use the pestle to grind the herbs in a doesil direction. Charge the powder by chanting the following charm while grinding:

Through the Goddess and the God;

Through the Moon and the Sun;

Through the elementals and planets;

Through the runes and the herbs;

With the power and blessings of Hera;

This powdered incense prompts love and agreement in marriage (relationship)!

So mote it be.

Place the powder in the bottle. Leave the bottle on the pentacle for one hour.

Snuff the candles, release the elementals and take down your circle.

Burn the incense on charcoal as needed.

Heal After Ending a Relationship

Sometimes when a relationship ends you need to find a semblance of peace. Even though the love is over you can still be civil to each other if not actual friends. You can use this spell for healing after a break up or a divorce. The best time to cast this spell is on a Monday during the full or new moon.

Spell ingredients:

1 blue candle

1 yellow candle

Cypress essential oil

Picture of the two of you in happier times

To cast the spell:

Cast your circle and invite the quarters.

Anoint both candles with the essential oil rubbing from the top to the bottom.

Place the candles on your altar and light them. Place the picture of the two of you between the candles.

Spend a little time thinking about all of the qualities you like in the other person.

Let go of any anger or resentment and then repeat
the incantation:

>Once together, now apart

>Time will mend a broken heart

>Help the seeds of "like" survive

>Even though love could not thrive

Help us put aside the past

>Let forgiveness come at last

>For the sake of those we hold dear

>Let us to the peace adhere

So mote it be.

Thank the quarters and close the circle.

Allow the candles to burn out safely.

Reunite Lovers

Many times a relationship ends before it is meant to. If the love is true and meant to be, you can bring your ex back to you. This spell is a good way to help you reunite with a lost lover. The best time to cast this spell is on a Friday during a full or new moon.

Spell ingredients:

1 pink candle

1 tablespoon coriander seeds

1 tablespoon poppy seeds

1 tablespoon of dried basil

3 drops Jasmine oil

1 stick vanilla incense

1 piece parchment paper

1 pink ink pen

Matches

Cauldron or fire proof dish

To cast the spell:

Cast your circle and invite the quarters.

Light the pink candle and place it in the center, but in the back, of your altar.

Light the vanilla incense from the candle and place it on the right side of the altar.

Write your name and the name of your lover on the parchment paper with the pink ink pen. Place it in the center of your altar.

Drip seven drops of wax on top of the names while visualizing your lover returning to you.

Place the coriander and poppy seeds, along with the basil on top of the wax.

Add three drops of the Jasmine oil to the mixture on the paper.

Again drip seven drops of wax on top of the mixture. See your lover returning and focus on giving your relationship another chance.

Fold the parchment paper seven times making sure to trap all of the ingredients inside.

Place the paper with the mixture in the cauldron and light it on fire. Allow it burn itself out.

Thank and release the quarters then close the circle.

Take the ashes from the cauldron and dispose of them in a moving body of water like a stream or river.

Strengthening the Bond

If you are in a loving relationship but feel the need to make it more secure, you can use this spell to accomplish that. This spell is best cast on a Friday during a full moon. The optimal time to perform the spell is between ten and eleven that night.

Spell ingredients:

A photograph of the two of you together (if you do not have one together, then two photographs, one of each individual, will work)

2 pink candles

Bouquet of white carnations

Flower vase

Mirror

To cast the spell:

You can perform this spell either inside or outside. Set your altar up so that it faces the moon.

First create your sacred space if you are working outside.

Cast the circle and invite the quarters.

Place the photograph of the two of you in the center of the altar. If using two pictures, place them side by side.

Set the pink candles on either side of the photograph/photographs.

Light the candles while focusing on the benefits of your relationship.

Place the carnations in the vase and set the vase on the altar behind the pictures.

Hold the mirror in your hand so that you can see a reflection of the photograph. Repeat the following incantation three times:

> I am bound to you
>
> You are bound to me
>
> I declare our love is true.
>
> This love is not obscure
>
> Blessed by the Goddess
>
> Make our love secure.

Snuff out the candles.

Thank the quarters and release them, then close the circle.

Keep your Lover Faithful

Infidelity is the number one cause of breakups in a relationship. No matter how much you love, someone there is always a chance they may cheat on you. The best way to keep your lover faithful is to have an honest, trusting relationship. But just in case you feel the need, here is a simple spell to help keep your lover faithful to you. The best time to cast this spell is on Friday, but a Monday would work well too.

Spell ingredients:

1 white candle

2 red candles

Large red heart cut from construction paper

Picture of you and a picture of your lover

Good quality ink pen

To cast the spell:

This spell takes seven days from beginning to end so be sure to plan ahead.

Cast your circle and invite the quarters.

Take the red heart and the pen and on the back write out what it is you wish or desire. Be sure to be very specific here so that you will get exactly what you want.

Place the white candle on the left side of the altar. If you are married, call upon the Goddess Hera, if you are in a love relationship call upon the Goddess Venus. Light the white candle to represent the Goddess.

Read your wishes and desires out loud to the Goddess.

Place the photographs, side by side, in the center of the altar. Then put the red heart on top of the pictures.

Place the red candles on either side of the pictures about one foot apart.

Light the candles and allow to burn for seven minutes. Concentrate on your desires.

After seven minutes, move the red candles slightly closer to each other and snuff out.

Thank the quarters and close the circle.

On day two, cast your circle and light the candles. Again allow them to burn for seven minutes. After seven minutes, move them closer together and snuff out. Close the circle.

You should repeat these steps for seven days. By the end of the spell the candles should be touching the pictures and the heart. On the last day allow the candles to burn out. Keep the pictures and heart in a safe place.

Overcome Jealousy

Jealousy can cause a lot of damage to a good relationship. Not only does it take up a lot of your energy, it creates tension and distrust between you and your partner. If jealousy is causing havoc in your relationship use this spell to overcome those feelings. The spell is best cast on a Saturday or Sunday during a dark or new moon.

Spell ingredients:

1 black or white candle

Lavender essential oil

To cast the spell:

It is not necessary to cast a circle before performing this spell.

Ground and center yourself. Anoint the candle by rubbing the essential oil from the bottom to the top.

Take a few deep breaths and then visualize yourself letting go of the jealous feelings. Focus on seeing the green-eyed monster leaving your body and walking away.

When you are ready, light the candle and repeat the incantation out loud in a firm voice:

Green-eyed monster

Get thee gone

I deny thee

And they power.

Jealousy I banish thee

From my relationship

From my heart

And from my spirit.

From this time forth

Let there be honesty

Let there be trust

And let love rule.

Green-eyed monster

Get thee done

I deny thee

And they power.

So mote it be.

Let the candle burn itself out in a safe place.

Letting Go

Whenever we lose a partner that we loved, it can leave a hole in our heart. You might feel like you will never love or trust anyone again. If you have experienced a recent break-up, you can use this spell to help heal the hurt it caused. This spell is best cast on a Saturday or Sunday during the waning moon.

Spell ingredients:

1 large white candle

2 small candles, 1 to represent each person

Length of yarn or cord

Scissors

To cast the spell:

Light the large white candle and place in the center of your altar. Place the smaller candles on each side of the large one.

Tie a knot in the cord.

Repeat the incantation:

> Once there was loving and joining

Bonds were made and vows were sworn

But all things have an ending

And what was whole has now been torn.

Today I let go of what was

So we might both move on to what might be

Without anger or regret

I gently set my old love free.

Love is never wasted or lost

And so I am grateful for all I had

All that I learned and felt

Although the outcome might be sad.

Today is a new day

And so I let go of sorrow and strife

Leaving only love and acceptance

As we both move on to a brand new life.

Light the smaller candles off of the large candle then snuff the large one out.

Use the scissors to cut the cord. Allow the smaller candles to burn out.

Mend Your Broken Heart

The end of a relationship is almost always painful. It can feel as if your heart is breaking. Losing a loved one is hard and getting over them takes time. To help speed up this process you can use this spell. It will help to mend your broken heart and allow you to be open to love again. This spell is best cast on a Sunday during the full or new moon.

Spell ingredients:

Piece of red or pink fabric

Scissors

Paper

Red or pink felt pen

Glue

1 green candle

1 stick of lavender incense

To cast the spell:

Cast your circle and call the quarters.

Light the incense and breathe in the peaceful energy of lavender.

Draw a heart on the paper and then cut out another heart, of the same size, from the fabric.

Think about the things that have hurt your heart, cutting a piece from the fabric heart as you do so.

When you are finished cutting up the fabric heart take a deep breath and look at all of the pieces.

Light the green candle and repeat:

By my magic and by my love

I mend my fractured heart.

Glue the fabric pieces onto the paper heart. Fill in any spaces with the ink pen. Concentrate on mending your heart and emotions.

Hold the mended heart to your own heart and repeat:

Patch and healed, love revealed.

Thank the quarters and close the circle.

Allow the candle to burn out in a safe place.

Keep the mended heart someplace safe as a reminder that you can heal and love again.

Break a love Spell

Getting rid of a lover that was brought to you through magic will need to be removed with magic. If you have cast a love spell that went awry, use this spell to break it. You will need a written copy of the original love spell. Handwrite it on a piece of paper or print it out from your computer. Cast this spell on a Friday during a waning moon.

Spell ingredients:

1 gray candle

Copy of original spell

White paint

To cast the spell:

Cast your circle and call the quarters.

Paint a white X across the copy of the original love spell and place it in the center of your altar.

Put the gray candle in a holder and set it on top of the original love spell.

While concentrating on the problems that the original spell has created in your life, light the candle.

When you are done with your visualizing the problems remove them by repeating the following chant three times:

> Love created through magic
>
> Is a false love, and I cast
>
> It away.

I neutralize the effects my

> Spell has caused and bring
>
> Healing instead today.

Allow the candle to burn out completely. Make sure it is in a safe location to do so.

Release the quarters and close the circle.

When the candle is completely burned out, roll up the remaining wax in the spell.

Dispose of all the ingredients in a trash dumpster. Preferably one that is not located in your own neighborhood.

You may repeat this spell as needed until the other person is gone from your life.

About the Author

Shawna Sparlin is a domestic goddess living in Tennessee. She is a single mother with one son still at home. Shawna has been working as a freelance writer for over five years. She has a number of published articles on the internet relating to parenting a child with Autism. Shawna has been a practicing Wiccan for the last thirty years. Other books include 25 All Natural Cough & Cold Remedies and Younger Skin in 30 Days or Less. If you would like information on where to find some of the ingredients listed in this book, or to ask her any questions you might have, you can reach her at shawnas@hushmail.com.

www.ingramcontent.com/pod-product-compliance
Lightning Source LLC
Chambersburg PA
CBHW071847020426
42331CB00007B/1902